What happens when you

TOUCH AND FEEL?

WHAT HAPPENS WHEN ...?

What Happens When You Breathe?
What Happens When You Catch a Cold?
What Happens When You Eat?
What Happens When You Grow?
What Happens When You Hurt Yourself?
What Happens When You Listen?
What Happens When You Look?
What Happens When You Run?
What Happens When You Sleep?
What Happens When You Talk?
What Happens When You Think?
What Happens When You Touch and Feel?

Library of Congress Cataloging-in-Publication Data

Richardson, Joy.
  What happens when you touch and feel?
  (What happens when — ?)
  Bibliography: p.
  Includes index.
  Summary: Describes how the body sends messages to the brain registering touch and sensation.
  1. Touch—Juvenile literature.   2. Senses and sensation—Juvenile literature. [1. Touch. 2. Senses and sensation]   I. Maclean, Colin, 1930-   ill.   II. Maclean, Moira, ill.   III. Title.   IV. Series: Richardson, Joy. What happens when— ?
QP450.R53 1986   612'.88   86-3679
ISBN 1-55532-139-9
ISBN 1-55532-114-3 (lib. bdg.)

This North American edition first published in 1986 by
Gareth Stevens, Inc.
7317 West Green Tree Road   Milwaukee, Wisconsin 53223, USA

U.S. edition, this format, copyright © 1986
Supplementary text and illustrations copyright © 1986
by Gareth Stevens, Inc.
Illustrations copyright © 1985 by Colin and Moira Maclean

First published in the United Kingdom by Hamish Hamilton Children's Books with an original text copyright by Joy Richardson.

Typeset by Ries Graphics, ltd.
Series editor: MaryLee Knowlton
Cover design: Gary Moseley
Additional illustration/design: Laurie Shock

What happens when you

TOUCH AND FEEL?

Joy Richardson

pictures by
Colin and Moira Maclean

introduction by
Gail Zander, Ph.D.

Gareth Stevens Publishing
Milwaukee

... a note to parents and teachers

Curiosity about the body begins shortly after birth when babies explore with their mouths. Gradually children add to their knowledge through sight, sound, and touch. They ask questions. However, as they grow, confusion or shyness may keep them from asking questions, and they may acquire little knowledge about what lies beneath their skin. More than that, they may develop bad feelings about themselves based on ignorance or misinformation.

The *What Happens When ...?* series helps children learn about themselves in a way that promotes healthy attitudes about their bodies and how they work. They learn that their bodies are systems of parts that work together to help them grow, stay well, and function. Each book in the series explains and illustrates how one of the systems works.

With the understanding of how their bodies work, children learn the importance of good health habits. They learn to respect the wonders of the body. With knowledge and acceptance of their bodies' parts, locations, and functions, they can develop a healthy sense of self.

This attractive series of books is an invaluable source of information for children who want to learn clear, correct, and interesting facts about how their bodies work.

GAIL ZANDER, Ph.D.
CHILD PSYCHOLOGIST
MILWAUKEE PUBLIC SCHOOLS

Is the water cold?

Is the package heavy?

Is the towel dry?

Is the pillow soft?

You cannot tell by looking,
but you can find out by feeling.

If you pet a cat,
it feels warm and soft and furry.
Your nerves carry messages
to your brain about it.

Under your skin there are
long thin threads called nerves.
Your nerves pick up feelings
and carry them to your brain.

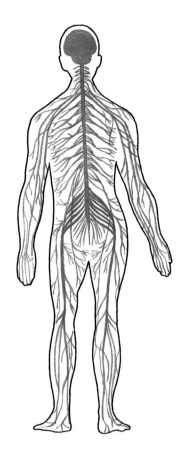

The messages start from
the nerve endings in your skin.
The nerve endings pass the messages
along the nerves into your backbone.
There are special nerves inside
your backbone which carry the messages
up to your brain.

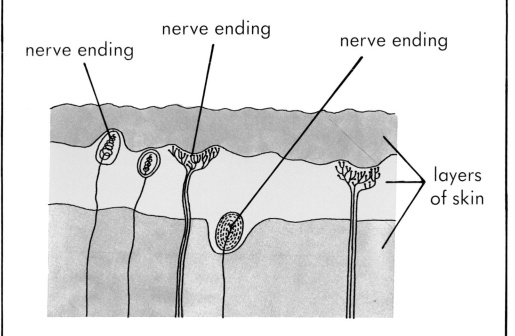

nerve ending

nerve ending

nerve ending

layers
of skin

The nerve endings in your skin
are different shapes.
They can pick up feelings
of hot or cold
or pressing or touching or hurting.

Your skin has two layers.
The nerve endings are
in the inside layer.
You cannot see them, but
you can feel them working.

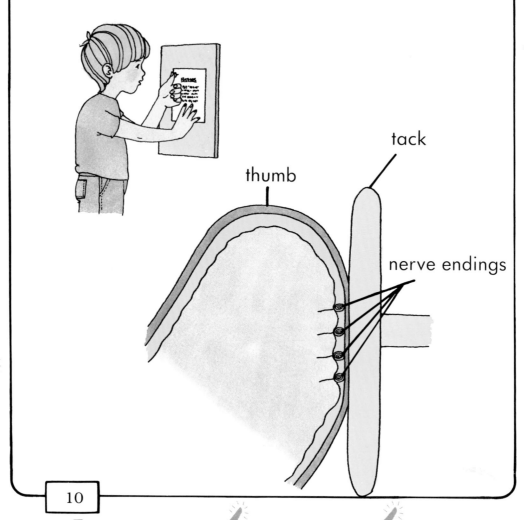

thumb

tack

nerve endings

Sit down and close your eyes.
Ask a friend to touch
different parts of your skin
(hand, nose, ear, and so on)
lightly with a pencil.

Tell where you can feel the touch.

There are nerve endings
all over your skin.

Fasten two pencils together
with a rubber band.
Close your eyes and press the points
on different parts of your skin.
Where can you feel
the two points most clearly?

Your hands and lips pick up
feelings clearly because the nerve
endings are very close together.

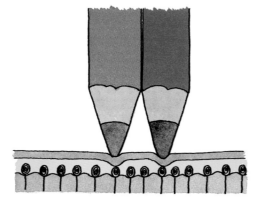

The nerve endings are further apart
in your arms and legs
and on your front and back.
So the feelings are less clear.

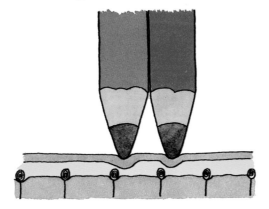

Put a piece of paper down
on a table in front of you.
Close your eyes.
Try to feel your way along
the edge of the paper with

your wrist,
your fingernail,
your knuckle,
your fingertip.

You can feel best of all
with your fingertips.
There are thousands of nerve endings
in each one.

People who are blind cannot see.
But they can find out
about things by feeling them.

Ask a friend to put
six things into a bag.
Close your eyes and stick
your hand into the bag.
Can you guess each thing
by feeling its shape?

You can find out a lot
with your fingertips.
The nerve endings can tell
if things feel rough or smooth,
or hard or soft,
or fluffy or sticky or slippery.

Collect some things made of wood,
metal, paper, plastic, cardboard, and cloth.
Blindfold a friend.
Let her feel a small part
of each thing with her fingertips.
Can she figure out
what it is made of?

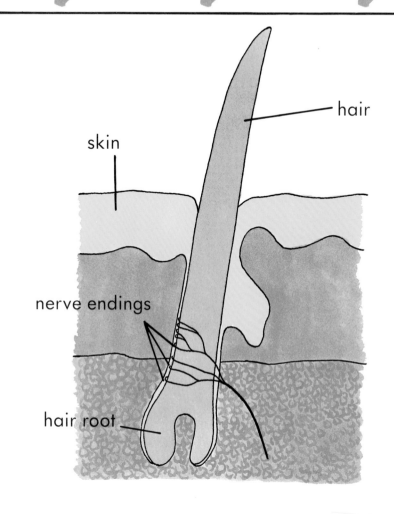

skin

hair

nerve endings

hair root

Your hair grows from
roots in your skin.
There are nerve endings
around the roots of your hair.
When a hair moves,
the nerve endings feel it.

Run your fingers lightly
over the hair on your head.
Pick up one hair and pull it.

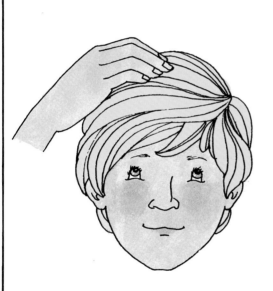

Nerve endings around the hair roots feel
the touch when you stroke your hair.
They feel the pain when you pull it.

Your mouth not only tastes your food,
but feels it, too.

Nerve endings in your mouth
can tell if cornflakes
are crunchy or soggy.
They can tell if pudding
is lumpy or smooth.

Take a bite of a cookie.
What does it feel like
to begin with?
What does it feel like
when you have chewed it up?

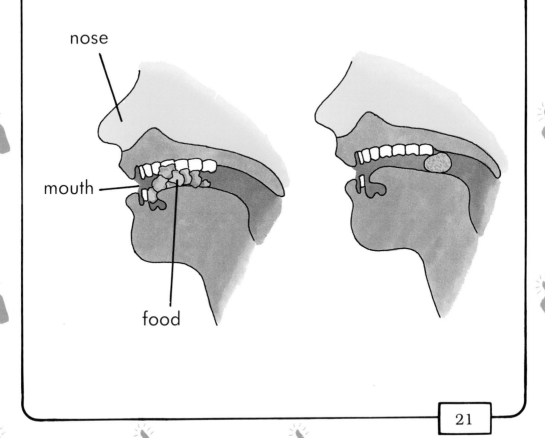

nose

mouth

food

When your nerve endings
pick up a new feeling,
they send urgent messages
to your brain about it.
When they get used to the feeling,
the messages slow down.

You feel your clothes when you
first put them on, but you
soon stop noticing the feeling.

Put on a hat and
keep reading.
You feel the hat to begin with,
but you soon get used to it.

Put your hand into cold water
and count to twenty.
The water feels less cold
once you get used to it.

Your nerves help to keep you safe.
If you touch something hot,
nerve endings in your skin
feel the pain.
The pain warns you to move away.

Messages travel along your nerves,
like telephone messages along a wire.

Messages from the nerve endings
in your skin take less than
a second to reach your brain.

If you prick your finger badly,
a pain message rushes along
nerves into your backbone.
Inside your backbone it triggers off
a message to your brain, and
an action message to your muscles.

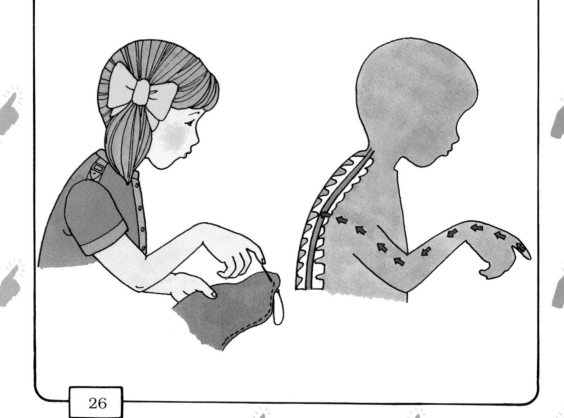

The action message travels along nerves
to the muscles in your arm.
It makes you pull your hand away.

When the message reaches your brain,
you start to think about the pain.

27

Some nerves pick up feelings
from the inside parts of your body.
They know if you have a stomach ache,
or if you are hungry or thirsty.

Your nerves tell your brain
how you are feeling,
inside and out.

How Does That Happen?

Did you find all these things to do in *What Happens When You TOUCH AND FEEL?* If not, turn back to the pages listed here and have some fun seeing how your body works.

1. *How do things feel?* (page 6)
2. *Have somebody touch you.* (page 11)
3. *See where you are most sensitive.* (page 12)
4. *See what part of your hand is most sensitive.* (page 14)
5. *Guess what things are just by feeling them.* (page 15)
6. *Guess what something is just by feeling it.* (page 17)
7. *Pull out a hair!* (page 19)
8. *How does a cookie feel in your mouth?* (page 21)
9. *See how your body gets used to a feeling.* (page 23)

More Books About
Touching and Feeling

Listed below are more books about what happens when you touch and feel. If you are interested in them, check your library or bookstore.

Beginning to Learn about Touching. Allington/Cowles (Raintree)

Find Out By Touching. Showers (Harper & Row)

From Head to Toes: How Your Body Works. Packard (Simon & Schuster)

Touch. Catherall (Silver Burdett)

The Touch Book. Moncure (Childrens Press)

Touch Will Tell. Brown (Franklin Watts)

What's Skin For? Blakely (Creative Education)

Where to Find More
About Touching and Feeling

Here are some people you can write away to for more information about what happens when you touch and feel. Be sure to tell them exactly what you want to know about. Include your full name and address so they can write back to you.

United Cerebral Palsy Associations, Inc.
66 East 34th Street
New York, New York 10016

Index

M
Mouth   20-21

N
Nerve endings   8-11, 13-14, 16, 18-20, 24-25

P
Pain   19, 24, 26-27

S
Skin   7-12, 18, 24-25

B
Backbone   8, 26
Blindness   15
Brain   7-8, 25-28

F
Fingertips   14, 16-17

H
Hair   18, 19